Harley-Davidson Motorcycles

By Eric Preszler

Consultant:
Amy Dukes
Marketing Director
Mike's Famous Harley-Davidson
　　　Museum of the American Road
New Castle, Delaware

Capstone
press

Mankato, Minnesota

Capstone High-Interest Books are published by Capstone Press
151 Good Counsel Drive, P.O. Box 669, Mankato, Minnesota 56002
www.capstonepress.com

Library of Congress Cataloging-in-Publication Data
Preszler, Eric.
　　Harley-Davidson motorcycles / by Eric Preszler.
　　　p. cm.— (Wild rides!)
　　Summary: Provides an overview of the history and development of
Harley-Davidson motorcycles, their main features, and motorcycle
competitions.
　　Includes bibliographical references and index (p. 32).
　　ISBN 0-7368-2429-4
　　1. Harley-Davidson motorcycle—History—Juvenile literature.
[1. Harley-Davidson motorcycle. 2. Motorcycles.] I. Title. II. Series.
TL448.H3P74 2004
629.227'5—dc22　　　　　　　　　　　　　　　　　　　　　　2003014554

Editorial Credits

James Anderson, editor; Kia Adams, series designer; Patrick D. Dentinger,
　　book designer; Jo Miller, photo researcher

Photo Credits

AP Wide World Photos/Damian Dovarganes, 28
Capstone Press/Gary Sundermeyer, cover
Corbis/Bettmann, 25; Ed Kashi, 4; Minnesota Historical Society, 10;
　　Underwood & Underwood, 22
Folio Inc., 6–7; Matthew Borkoski, 19
Getty Images/AFP, 20; Vanina Lucchesi, 8; Daniel Berehulak, 12; David
　　McNew, 26
Transparencies Inc./Jane Faircloth, 14, 17, 18

1　2　3　4　5　6　09　08　07　06　05　04

Table of Contents

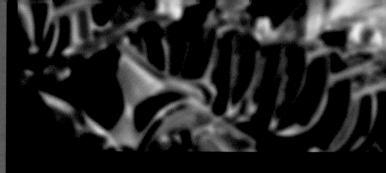

Learn about:

- **Sturgis Motorcycle Rally**

- **American-made motorcycles**

- **Costs**

CHAPTER 1

A Motorcycle Legend

Thousands of Harley-Davidson motorcycles cruise along the interstates and highways. The smell of pine trees from the Black Hills of South Dakota fills the air as the bikers glide through the countryside. The motorcycles' chrome shines off store windows as bikers drive into a busy small town.

The bikers arrive for a weeklong event that many Harley-Davidson riders dream about. It is called the Sturgis Motorcycle Rally. About 300,000 riders come from all over the world to the small South Dakota town of Sturgis. The bikers do not mind the hot August temperatures. The rally is one of the largest meetings of motorcycle riders in the world.

About Harley-Davidson Motorcycles

To many people, the name Harley-Davidson stands for the freedom of the open road and a sense of adventure. Many Harley-Davidson owners are proud that their motorcycles are made in the United States. Harley-Davidson is the only active major U.S. motorcycle maker. The popularity of Harley-Davidson motorcycles helped the company earn the 2001 Company of the Year Award from *Forbes* magazine.

Many people are willing to pay a great deal of money for the excitement of a Harley. The average cost is $15,000. But prices can easily reach at least $25,000 if many accessories are added. New Harleys can cost from $6,000 for a basic model to $22,000 for a model with extra parts and accessories. Some collectible Harleys cost more than $50,000.

Many Harley riders enjoy the freedom of motorcycle riding.

Sidecars offer a fun way for riders to carry passengers.

Harleys in Action

Throughout the last 100 years, Harley-Davidson motorcycles have served many purposes. During World War II (1939–1945), some U.S. soldiers rode Harleys. The soldiers easily moved the motorcycles to different locations.

Today, some police officers ride motorcycles because they move swiftly through traffic. Police have used Harley-Davidsons for many years. The first Harley-Davidsons were faster than the first cars. It was easy for police officers on Harleys to catch speeding drivers.

Many riders use their motorcycles to travel around the country. Most Harley-Davidsons are built to carry two people. Saddlebags make it easy for travelers to carry more supplies. Saddlebags are leather bags attached to the sides of a motorcycle near the rear wheel.

Some riders race motorcycles. Harleys are popular motorcycles in endurance events and drag races.

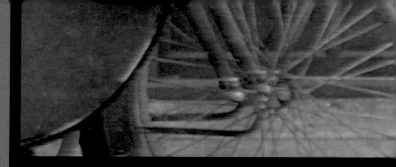

Learn about:

- The Davidson basement

- The "Silent Gray Fellow"

- Clutch motorcycles

CHAPTER **2**

GUY W. WEBB
MOTORCYCLES

Early Harleys

The Harley-Davidson Company began in 1903 when four young men in Milwaukee, Wisconsin, added a gas engine to a bicycle. William Harley, and brothers Arthur, Walter, and William Davidson worked in the basement of the Davidson house. The first Harley-Davidson motorcycle was called Serial Number One. As they built more motorcycles, they moved their shop to a small shed.

Serial Number One

During the early 1900s, many Americans wanted to see and explore their country. Very few people owned cars. The main ways to travel were on horses, bicycles, and trains. Harley and the Davidson brothers believed they had found a better way to travel.

Some of the first Harley-Davidson
motorcycles are now on display
in museums.

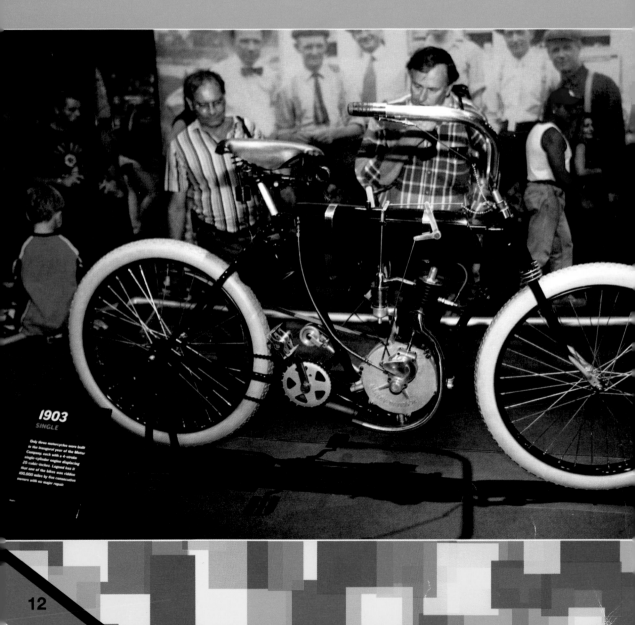

1903
SINGLE

Only three motorcycles were built
in the inaugural year of the Motor
Company, each with a 4-stroke
single-cylinder engine displacing
25 cubic inches. Legend has it
that one of the bikes was ridden
100,000 miles by five consecutive
owners with no major repair.

Serial Number One and other early Harleys had bike pedals. Riders had to pedal the bike to start the engine. These bikes were dull gray in color and very quiet. They moved slowly. Some people called the first Harleys the "Silent Gray Fellow."

Early Changes

In 1912, Harley-Davidson started to sell motorcycles with a clutch. The clutch allowed riders to shift gears and increase speed. With more than one gear, Harleys could go faster and were more powerful.

Around this time, Harley-Davidson also began selling motorcycles with sidecars. This addition allowed riders to safely carry an extra passenger or more supplies. People began riding Harleys on long trips.

Learn about:

- V-Twin engine
- Choppers
- Gold paint

CHAPTER 3

Designing and Customizing a Harley

Harley-Davidson motorcycles are often thought of as powerful and unique. The V-Twin engine makes the bikes powerful. Many Harley-Davidson riders have made changes to their motorcycles to make them unique.

Riding a Harley

Harleys have three main controls on the handlebars. The throttle is located on the right handlebar. It controls speed. The front brake is also on the right handlebar. Pulling the brake lever controls the front brake. The clutch is on the left handlebar. Riders pull the clutch lever with their left hand. They shift gears with their left foot.

Like other motorcycles, Harleys have two main controls near the footpegs. These pegs are where a rider's feet rest. The rear brake lever is in front of the right footpeg. Riders push down on the lever with their toes to control the rear brake.

The gear lever is on the left side. Riders push the gear lever all the way down to shift into first gear. Pulling it up with the toe raises the gear. All Harley-Davidsons have five gears. The highest gears are used for high speeds.

A U.S. law passed in 1975 says that both the clutch and the gear lever must be on the same side of the motorcycle. The front and rear brakes are on the other side. Motorcycles are easy and safe to ride when both brakes are on the same side.

Harley-Davidson motorcycles have a gear lever near the left footpeg.

Two cylinders come together in a *V* shape on a V-Twin engine.

Engine

Harley-Davidson engines have two cylinders where fuel is burned. The burned fuel creates the power to move the motorcycle.

The Harley-Davidson's V-Twin engine sets it apart from other motorcycle companies. It is called V-Twin because the two cylinders come together in the shape of a *V*.

V-Twin engines are loud. They give Harleys a unique sound. When several Harleys cruise along a highway at the same time, some people say the sound is like thunder.

Harley-Davidsons are well known for their loud V-Twin engines.

Customizing

Most Harley riders want motorcycles that fit their personalities. Making changes and additions to motorcycles is called customizing. With different parts, riders can add a personal touch to their motorcycles. Some Harley styles fit the toughness of their riders. Other styles are designed for comfortable travel.

Some riders like their Harleys to look unique and express their personality.

Almost any part of a Harley can be customized in some way. The design of the wheels can be changed. The engine's power can be increased. A longer fork can be added. The fork connects the front wheel to the handlebars. Motorcycles with long forks are called choppers. Some choppers have the original front wheel. Other choppers have smaller front wheels.

Many riders create their own gas tank designs. Some paints used to customize Harleys contain shiny metal shavings. This paint is called metallic paint. Some metallic paint contains real gold shavings. Some riders have flames painted on the gas tanks of their Harleys.

Learn about:

CHAPTER **4**

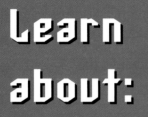

Harleys in Competition

The Harley-Davidson company started racing motorcycles in 1908. The company wanted to prove that their motorcycles were reliable. They entered long-distance races that tested a motorcycle's endurance. These races are called enduros. Harley-Davidson riders won the first race they entered. This race was a two-day, 365-mile (587-kilometer) event.

Harley-Davidson riders were successful in many early races that they entered. Because of many wins at racetracks, Harley-Davidson's sales increased. People began to think of Harleys as powerful motorcycles.

Speed

By 1909, the focus of motorcycle racing had turned to speed. Bikers started reaching speeds of 100 miles (160 kilometers) an hour or more. The Harley-Davidson racing team became known as the "Wrecking Crew" because people said they wrecked their opponents' chances of winning.

The first speed races took place on board tracks. These tracks were large ovals made of wood. Riders who fell from their bikes often got splinters from these tracks. By the late 1920s, most races were moved to dirt tracks.

Famous Racers

Harley-Davidson racer Joe Petrali was a legend of the dirt track. In 1935, he won all 13 races on the national schedule. He set a speed record of 136.18 miles (219.16 kilometers) an hour in 1937.

Scott Parker joined the Harley-Davidson racing team in 1981. Parker won nine Grand National Champion titles in 10 years. Most people consider Parker the most successful racer in Harley-Davidson history.

Joe Petrali, seated center, was one of the first Harley-Davidson racers.

Drag Racing

Drag racing is a popular form of motorcycle racing. Many auto racetracks have motorcycle drag races. Most Harleys that are used in drag racing have been modified. These Harleys have traveled at speeds of up to 200 miles (320 kilometers) an hour.

Hill Climb

Hill climb races were most popular in the 1930s. In these events, riders race to the top of a steep hill.

Some hill climbs still take place today. Most are races between dirt bikes, not Harleys. People watch a hill climb at the Sturgis Motorcycle Rally each year.

Motorcycle Legend

Harley riders know that their motorcycles are special. They are proud of the company's long history in the United States. They know that Harley-Davidson motorcycles will continue to be a motorcycle legend.

Hill climb races still take place each year at the Sturgis Motorcycle Rally.

The VRSC V-Rod

The VRSC V-Rod is the first member of a new family of Harley-Davidson motorcycles. The V-Rod is low to the ground. Its design is based on drag racing motorcycles.

The V-Rod is powered by a V-Twin Revolution engine. Harley-Davidson teamed up with Porsche to create the design for this new engine. The V-Twin Revolution can power the V-Rod to 140 miles (225 kilometers) an hour.

A new 2004 Harley-Davidson V-Rod costs about $18,000. Many custom options are available for the V-Rod. Buyers can change the bike's color or add other features. These features affect the cost of the V-Rod.

Glossary

chrome (KROHM)—a coating of a metallic substance called chromium; chrome gives objects a shiny metallic appearance.

clutch (KLUCH)—a part of a motorcycle that allows the rider to shift gears

cylinder (SIL-uhn-dur)—a tube inside an engine where gas is burned

modify (MOD-uh-fye)—to change

motorize (MOH-tur-ize)—to add a motor

throttle (THROHT-uhl)—a device that controls the flow of fuel into the engine; the throttle is located on a motorcycle's right handlebar.

Read More

Davidson, Willie G. *100 Years of Harley-Davidson.* Boston: Bulfinch Press, 2002.

Youngblood, Ed. *Dirt Track Racing.* Motorcycles. Mankato, Minn.: Capstone Press, 2000.

Useful Addresses

Harley-Davidson

Customer Service

3700 West Juneau Avenue

Milwaukee, WI 53208

Harley Owners Group

National H.O.G. Office

P.O. Box 453

Milwaukee, WI 53201

Internet Sites

FactHound offers a safe, fun way to find Internet sites related to this book. All of the sites on FactHound have been researched by our staff.

Here's how:

1. Visit *www.facthound.com*
2. Type in this special code **0736824294** for age-appropriate sites. Or enter a search word related to this book for a more general search.
3. Click on the **Fetch It** button.

FactHound will fetch the best sites for you!

Index